dream small

"Everyone deserves to find meaning in their work. But few books tell you how - until now."

"Jeff Hilimire's *Dream Small* is more than a book - it's an invitation to pause, reflect, and find meaning in the everyday moments of our lives and work. Through the beloved characters of the Turnaround Leadership Universe, Jeff masterfully weaves a story that is equal parts heartfelt, inspiring, and deeply personal.

What sets *Dream Small* apart is its honest exploration of how focusing on others - on their growth, well-being, and success - can lead to a life of extraordinary purpose and fulfillment. It's not a typical leadership book; it's a life book, one that gently reminds us to look inward while staying rooted in service to others.

With poignant lessons, rich storytelling, and a dash of humor, Jeff proves once again why his words resonate so deeply with his readers. This is a book for anyone seeking to make a difference, both in the lives they touch and in their own personal journey. *Dream Small* reminds us that the greatest transformations often come from the simplest, most intentional steps."

"Jeff Hilimire has created a beautiful series that is informative, entertaining, easy to read, and one I have grown to love. But this book in particular holds so much more depth and emotion as it wrestles with loss and deepens your connection with the characters. I laughed, cried, and feel incredibly honored to be a part of this book that will inspire people to discover their purpose work."

ASHLEY NICOLE JONES,
founder of Momento Foundation and author of When You Can't See the Light

dream small

The Secret to Finding Meaning in Work and Life

jeff hilimire

Ripples Media

Cover design by Corey Davis
Interior typesetting by Najdan Mancic

First printing 2025

979-8-9913870-3-3 Paperback
979-8-9913870-4-0 Ebook

Published by Ripples Media
ripples.media

To Emily. Thank you for allowing me to chase my dreams and find meaning and fulfillment in my work . . . and also for that loving me unconditionally part.

And to Gina Gentilozzi, who was as big a part of building 48in48 as anyone, and who showed me that dreaming small can pay huge dividends. We miss you dearly.

*Every generation inherits a world
it never made; and, as it does so, it
automatically becomes the trustee of
that world for those who come after.*

BOBBY KENNEDY

Life is a journey, not a destination.

PRESIDENT JIMMY CARTER

CONTENTS

PREAMBLE

Thank you for choosing this book. There are so many books published each year and far too few hours to read them, so the fact that you've chosen to read this book means a lot. It really does.

Dream Small is set in the Turnaround Leadership Universe (TLU). Thus, the main characters in this book will be familiar to followers of that series. After writing my first book, *The 5-Day Turnaround*, I just haven't been able to break away from these quirky characters. They've become friends I look forward to visiting each time I start a new book.

What's unique about this book, for me, is that it's not exactly a leadership book. It's what I might call a "life" book, with the goal of inspiring readers (you!) to create a better life for themselves, and at the same time ideally making the world a better place for others. In my experience, the more one focuses on the latter, the more the former begins to take shape.

Perhaps I've said all I need to say about leadership with my first five books (doubtful), but at this point, I'm more interested in sharing experiences I've had that have helped me create what I would consider an incredibly blessed and fulfilled life.

So, let's dive in.

PROLOGUE

Our story starts with two men sitting on a bench in a park. (And, not to foreshadow too much, but that's precisely how it will end.)

But this isn't just any old park. This particular park is one that the older man helped design over twenty years ago. And, the younger man's (though he's pushing fifty at this point, so "younger" perhaps isn't the best way to describe him) marketing agency helped to name the park.

The two men, however, aren't talking about the park's creation or its name (Foothills Park, solid if not inspiring branding work). They're talking about what they talk about most of the time when they get together, usually about three to four times a year. They're talking about the younger man's problems.

The older man (Charles) has been mentoring the younger man (Will) since their first meeting. Like he's doing right now.

"I don't know," Will said, kicking some rocks under his feet. "I just kind of feel . . . stuck. For the first time, I'm unsure which direction to head with my career."

"Could this have anything to do with Danni starting college last month?" Charles asked. Danni, as Charles affectionately calls her, is Will's daughter. Charles has always doted on Danni, and recently served as a very impactful reference for her college applications.

Will nodded. "Oh, I'm sure that hasn't helped. It was tough for Sarah and me when Danielle left the house, but luckily, she's only an hour away. In fact, we've already visited her for a weekend."

Much to her chagrin. It wasn't that Danielle didn't like seeing her parents - she did - but to visit within the first month of school seemed a tad . . . eager. She was willing to go to a school close to home under the condition that her parents not pretend she was still living at home. A condition they were, one month in, already close to violating.

"As you know, I've been less essential to the agency ever since I promoted Rachel. Which is a good thing, don't get me wrong . . . and I've kind of run the gamut on the whole consulting and leadership book writing I've been doing," Will said. "And lately, I've been wondering what the point of it all is?"

Let me pause and point out a few things. First, as the storyteller, I will try my best to lay this narrative out without diving into the rest of the Turnaround Leadership Universe *(TLU). But occasionally, I'll point out something that happened in a previous book for context.*

In this case, during The Great Team Turnaround, *Will promoted Rachel to run his marketing agency, and then began working as a consultant and author/speaker. That book focuses on building a great team, though you might have guessed that from the title. Also, there's a talking robot.*

Back to our story.

Charles looked at his friend. "The point of all *what*, exactly?"

"Of life, maybe? I've been working for over 25 years, and I'm wondering what it's all for. Am I making a big enough impact? What will I be remembered for?"

Charles frowned. "You're not referring to your *legacy*, right? Because we've talked about that . . . "

"No, definitely not legacy," Will said, interrupting. "I know that's the wrong thing to be pursuing. You've beaten that into my head enough over the years."

Charles had strong opinions on someone's motivation in life being to secure their "legacy." He felt bad for people who put their need to be remembered reverently as their top goal in life. Not to mention that you won't be around to feel flattered by everyone fawning over your memory anyway.

"Good. So if it's not legacy, what are you finding hard to reconcile with?" Charles asked.

Will thought for a moment. "I guess I just hope that somehow the work I did during my life ends up being important or meaningful in some way. I know that sounds like the classic midlife crisis cliche, but has the work I've done made the world better in any way?

"And I've been thinking about things I could do that might be more meaningful - I have a notepad full of ideas - but I end up coming up with a lot of big ideas that feel too overwhelming to attempt."

Charles nodded. "Ah, I see. So you want to find more meaning in your work, and you are struggling to figure out how to do that, partly because the size and scope of your ideas are too grand."

"I think that's right, yeah," Will said. "Like, I want to make a *real* impact, you know?"

Before Charles could respond, they heard music coming toward them. "Sounds like our old friend is coming through. I'll let him go by before responding," he said.

"The Skateman," a somewhat famous character in their town, approached. Will thought he was somewhere between forty and sixty years old (The Skateman never shared his age), and most people didn't know his real name (Ricardo). He wore, as you might have derived from his clever moniker, a set of old-school roller skates. The rest of his ensemble was equally interesting: a pair of denim cut-off jeans, a fishnet T-shirt, several dozen fake Mardi Gras-style beaded necklaces, and a top hat best described as "full-on Mad Hatter." He was typically seen skating around town through-out the day, high-fiving people and dodging cars along the way.

Unfortunately for The Skateman, this partic-ular part of the path was made of loose rocks, re-quiring him to walk gingerly so his roller skates would not catch on any pebbles. He was using it as a cut-through between two concrete paths and was excited to see his two friends.

"Will and Charles, as I live and breathe!" he shouted over the music blaring from the boombox on his shoulder.

Will waved and motioned for him to lower the music by turning an invisible knob to the left with his hand. "Oh, right, it's too loud," The Skateman shouted, gesturing at the boombox. "I'll turn it down."

He came over to sit down, so Will shimmied clos-er to Charles to make room. The Skateman set the boombox on his lap and asked how they were doing.

"We're great," Will said. "Sorry that the conven-tion center took down your billboard. At least they kept it up a few weeks after the campaign." Will's agency had been hired to promote a massive con-ference in town last summer, and even though Will wasn't active in the agency at that point, he stayed involved due to his role on the city council. The

Skateman was brought on to the campaign after a research survey ranked him as one of the top ten most notable figures to look for while in town.

The Skateman shrugged. "Oh, no worries, I barely noticed it wasn't up anymore." He was too proud to admit that he had actually noticed the very moment they changed the billboard, as he made it a point to skate past it routinely while it was up.

Will wasn't fooled. "Swing by the agency next week if you get a chance. We have a box for you of posters and pins and stuff from the campaign with your face on them," he said as a big smile appeared on The Skateman's face.

While Will knew The Skateman through work, Charles knew him from the streets, as he often traveled through town by bicycle. In fact, almost every time Will and Charles had met at Foothills Park over the years, Charles was in cycling gear, typically with his helmet in his arms. He wasn't dressed like that on this day, a fact that Will had not yet noticed.

They caught up for a few more minutes before The Skateman asked, "So, what are you two talking about?"

Before Will could respond, Charles said, "Will isn't sure his work is important or meaningful. It's fortuitous that you came by because I'm guessing you could help shine some light on this."

The Skateman looked at the two of them, contemplating the question. "Well, first of all, I don't know what 'fortuitous' means; you college doctor-lawyers always use such big words," he chuckled. They were sure he overplayed his lack of education but never called him on it. "But, that *is* interesting to think about. Would I say my work is important? I should start by asking you two fine gentlemen what you think my work is."

It was generally understood by everyone in town that The Skateman's "work" was skating around town blasting music on his boombox, and Will indicated as much.

They heard someone yell, "Hey, Skateman!" A jogger approached them with a big grin. He reached out his hand for a high-five, which The Skateman happily returned, then kept running.

As they watched the jogger turn the corner and out of view, The Skateman pointed and said, "That. *That* is what I do, and his reaction is why I do it."

Will, a bit confused, asked him to elaborate. Only he didn't use the word 'elaborate' after the whole 'fortuitous' incident.

"Look, I used to have a nine-to-five job, and man, it sucked! Can you imagine me sitting behind a desk all day?" Predictably, they couldn't. "But once

I received my inheritance and didn't need to work anymore, I found my true calling."

Will had learned about The Skateman's cash windfall during their time working on the campaign together, so that part wasn't a surprise. But his . . . *calling*?

The Skateman continued. "You see, I've always been able to make people happy, simply by being me! And making people happy always makes *me* happier. So I leaned into that and eventually found myself about town, trying to cheer people up. Skating allowed me to cover more ground. Take that guy I just high-fived. He will be telling all his friends that he saw me today. His day will be at least a tiny bit better for that, and maybe he'll be friendlier or kinder to someone. Perhaps his smile will make someone else smile. And I did that!"

Just then, his watch buzzed. "OK, gentlemen, gotta go. There's supposed to be a minor picket line in front of the old Smith factory downtown. I know those folks are upset, and I'm going to try to cheer them up a bit."

He gave Will and Charles a fist bump, turned his music back up well beyond where it started, and made his way down the path.

"OK, that was helpful . . . I think." They couldn't see The Skateman any longer, but they could still hear him. Smiling, Will added, "Isn't there a noise ordinance or something in this park?"

"There sure is, but The Skateman is exempt, just like he apparently is from regular traffic rules," Charles said. "He marches to his own beat, but he seems pretty fulfilled in his work, doesn't he?"

"He *does* seem happy doing his 'work,'" Will said, putting air quotes around work. It was at this point that he realized Charles wasn't wearing cycling gear. "Charles, did you not bike here?"

"No, not today," he said.

It was a beautiful day, so Will thought he might have had a meeting after this. But something about his demeanor seemed off.

"Wait, you asked for this meeting, right?" Will asked. He couldn't remember a time when Charles had initiated one of their meetups. "I've just been yapping away as usual about my problems. What did you want to talk about?"

Charles looked down, unsure how to say what he needed to say. Perhaps it was because of the depth of their relationship and how much they both meant to each other. Perhaps it was because, well, how do you say these things anyway? *Best to be out with it*, he thought.

"Well, Will," he said, looking at him. "The thing is . . . I'm dying."

THE HOSPITAL

Six months later, Will found himself standing in the parking lot of Silver Cross Hospital, a relatively new hospital near Foothills Park.

He was struggling with the old-school parking meter and trying his third credit card when a nurse walking by noticed his struggle.

"Uh, honey," she said, getting Will's attention. "I think you have to flip it the other way around."

Will looked down at the card and, realizing his mistake, turned the card over and swiped it.

Sheepishly, he said, "Thank you. You'd think I'd have this figured out, given how many times I've visited this hospital lately. I guess I'm just a little distracted today."

"Don't worry, you're not the first to struggle with these old meters. I don't know why they don't upgrade them," she said. "You have someone in here you're visiting, I take it?"

"I do," he said, extending his hand for a fist bump.

She returned the first bump. Will glanced at her name badge. "Nice to meet you, Nurse Elizabeth. I'm Will."

"Nice to meet you as well, Will." Gesturing toward the path to the hospital, she asked, "Shall we?"

On the walk, Will learned that Nurse Elizabeth had worked at Silver Cross for over ten years, was a grandmother to two kids under the age of five, and was not a fan of laziness or messiness on the job. A point she made several times on their short walk, giving Will the impression that there were a few other nurses she'd like to give a talking to.

They entered the hospital, and she said, "Well, it's nice to meet you. I hope your friend gets out soon."

Will nodded. "Yeah. Me, too." He looked around to see if anyone could hear him and whispered, "And good luck with all those . . . lazy slobs you have to work with."

She laughed. Putting her finger to her lips she whispered, "That's our little secret," before disappearing down a hallway.

Will looked at the large map on the wall in the lobby. He had not been looking forward to today, as it would be Charles's first day in the hospice wing. Over the last six months, his cancer had progressed at an alarming rate, and Charles had been in and out of the hospital receiving treatments. That was until last week, when it was decided that it was time for hospice.

Charles didn't have any family, having lost his wife and son many years ago. Will's and Sarah's parents didn't live in the state, so their family had adopted Charles over the years as Danielle's surrogate grandfather, inviting him over for holidays and big events. He wasn't always able to attend - he was a very active and busy man, often traveling on cycling trips or other adventures - but he made it a point to be there for the truly important moments. And Danielle simply adored him. She was devastated when Will told her the news and had been to visit Charles several times during his treatments.

Figuring out the path to the hospice wing required many twists and turns, but thankfully, the hospital had various colored arrows on the floor to guide visitors to the right place. The instructions informed Will to follow the green arrow until he came to the pink arrow, which would lead him to the hospice wing. He thought he could manage that.

At the end of the day, though, he couldn't; he got lost more than one time. Like the parking meter, we'll blame it on his grief.

Eventually, he found the hospice wing and approached the nurse's counter, where he saw a familiar face.

"Oh . . . ," Nurse Elizabeth said softly, realizing that Will's friend was a terminal patient in her unit. "Hi, Will. I didn't realize . . . "

"It's OK," he replied. Behind Elizabeth, there was a big board with patients' names listed next to their rooms. Will quickly saw which room Charles was in. "Looks like my friend is in room 7A."

She looked behind her and said, "Oh, you're Charles's friend! I just came from his room. He checked in last night, and apparently, charmed all the other nurses. You're in luck. I'm assigned to him on the day shift." She looked around to see if anyone could hear and whispered, "And as we talked about on the way in, I'm the best nurse they've got."

Will laughed. "Oh, I don't doubt that." He looked around the nurses' station and added in a hushed tone, "And you're right, this place is a *pigsty*. I'm going to see if I can get Charles moved to another hospital this afternoon. This is completely unacceptable."

"I know, right? I'll print up a list of better options for you while you visit Charles," she grinned. "He's right down at the end of that hallway."

Will peered down the hallway, unable to move. He had been worried all morning about seeing Charles in this new setting, knowing it meant his time was truly limited. Any denial that Will was experiencing in the hopes that Charles would make a recovery was vanquished with the decision to move to hospice. And walking down this hallway was the physical embodiment of that realization.

He saw the door marked 7A with Charles's name on the dry-erase board next to the door. Dry-erase board, so it can easily be erased when Charles is gone, he thought.

He knocked on the door and heard Charles's voice say, "Who is it?"

"It's Dr. Rosenrosen," Will said.

He heard a chuckle inside, and then, "I'm sorry, Dr . . . .?"

"It's Dr. Rosen," Will replied.

Charles laughed again. "Ok, come on in, we best not follow that thread to the end."

I can forgive many things, but if you weren't able to follow Will and Charles's banter, you haven't seen (or, gasp, don't remember!) the movie Fletch *- one of the finest pieces of film (an affinity that Will and Charles share.) I give you permission to put this book down and watch the movie before continuing. There will be one more* Fletch *reference in this chapter; see if you can spot it.*

Will entered the room and was immediately struck by how bright it was. Light was streaming in from four large windows spanning just about from the floor to the ceiling. There was a nice-looking sofa to his left, and Charles was sitting up in his large, comfortable-looking bed to the right. A TV was on the wall opposite him, and next to the bed was what looked to be a leather recliner. Were it not for medical equipment to the right of Charles's bed (and perhaps that hospital smell we all know too well), you might have thought it was a regular living room.

"So," Charles asked, gesturing toward the room, "What do you think? Not bad, right?"

"No, not bad at all," Will said, noticing how raspy Charles's voice was. He approached the bed and shook Charles's hand. "But I thought I ordered the penthouse suite with the heart-shaped jacuzzi and velvet drapes. I'm going to have to talk with someone about that."

Charles's laugh quickly turned into a cough, and Will immediately regretted making the joke. He knew better, as Charles hadn't been able to laugh without coughing for many months.

Will grabbed the cycling magazine and *The New York Times* crossword puzzle book from the recliner seat and plopped down. He looked over at the tiny kitchen where most of the medical equipment was stored.

"Is that a fridge?" he asked, stalling. He didn't want to feel awkward visiting his old friend, but knowing this was the last room Charles would ever be in, the last bed he'd ever sleep in, just kind of hit him all at once.

"Yep, and it's fully stocked. Even though I told them I only drink water, they still threw some other stuff in there. Feel free to grab something if you're thirsty," he said.

At that moment, Nurse Elizabeth entered the room and walked over to the bed with her clipboard. She asked Charles a few questions, made some notes, and then asked Will if there was anything he needed to be more comfortable.

Will looked around the room and frowned. "To be honest, this place could use a good cleaning.

I'm a bit appalled at how disorganized everything is in here."

Charles's eyes went wide. "Will, I don't think..."

Without missing a beat, Nurse Elizabeth interrupted Charles. "Well, if you don't like it, you should take your friend over to Brady Hospital. From what I've heard, they specialize in handling their patients' more ... annoying visitors."

Will glanced at Charles, whose face had gone pale with shock. Charles looked back and forth at them ... and caught the tiniest smirk on Will's face.

"Wait a minute," he asked, "do you two know each other or something?"

Nurse Elizabeth and Will both burst out laughing. She said, "Oh yeah, we go way back ... to about an hour ago. He'd still be in the parking lot trying to pay the meter if it wasn't for me."

"True story," Will said. "I think you're in pretty good hands with this one, Charles."

As she left the room, Charles said, "Wow, you really had me for a minute."

A few moments paused between them, and Will finally asked, "So, for real, how *are* you doing?"

Charles sat up a bit more in bed, adjusting the pillows behind his back. The aggressive treatment his body had been through had made him weak - something he was not accustomed to.

"It's kind of an amazing thing," he said. "You know I'm a fighter . . . but when it was decided that there was nothing more to do to help me, that the cancer had progressed too far for the treatment to have much effect . . . an overall peace came over me. I never imagined myself in this situation, but now that I'm here, I'm actually okay with it."

Will, unable to hide his surprise, asked, "Really? You're not just saying that because you're worried about my feelings?"

Charles smiled at his friend. He knew how much Will cared about him, and he *would* have tried to hide his anxiety, but he truly had accepted his situation and was ready for whatever would come next.

"No, Will," Charles said. "I'm not just saying that."

"Okay, then I have to ask. How in the world are you so calm about this?"

Charles took a sip from the water bottle on the table next to his bed. "I've been thinking about that, and, if I can say this without sounding too . . . self-righteous, I feel like I've led a purposeful life. As I look back on the things I've done, how I've tried to treat people, perhaps even the impact I've had on others and the world around me . . . I feel content. I know I could have done more, but for the most part, I think I did a pretty decent job.

"I guess, what it boils down to is that I feel like I left the world a bit better during my lifetime. And perhaps that's all we can hope for."

Will could tell that Charles meant what he said. There was a peace within him; he could . . . sense it. Amazingly, his friend seemed *ready* for his time to come to an end.

"Which leads me to how I think I can help you with *your* problem," Charles said.

Of course, Will thought, when he was going through arguably the most difficult part of life a person can experience, Charles was more focused on helping others.

"Sorry, but what problem of mine are we talking about? There are so many . . ." Will responded, smiling.

Charles laughed and then coughed for a few minutes. "You really gotta stop doing that. I said I was at peace with dying; I didn't say I wanted to get there sooner than necessary!"

He took another sip of water and continued. "It's pretty clear to me that your major struggle right now is that you're not fulfilled in your work. Like it doesn't have enough meaning."

Will nodded, so Charles continued. "I've reflected on my life since I've been sick - time to think is just about the only benefit of being locked in here - and

I've realized the major reasons why I feel content with the life I lived."

"Wait, are you saying you have the . . . secret to life?" Will asked, smiling a little but also realizing that if someone *had* figured that out, it would be Charles. "If so, you should really write a book about that!"

I bet if someone did, it would be called The Life Turnaround.

Smiling, Charles said, "I feel like I have the major elements broken down to live a life worth living, yes. And one major component of that is finding purpose in your work. Which is what I think you're currently lacking. Unless you think I'm wrong?"

"No, as usual, I think you're spot on," Will said. "By all accounts, I've succeeded in what I've done. Heck, people literally pay me to talk about my career. But when I look back on it, I can't see how the work I've done has any meaning beyond helping me and my family."

Charles then explained that he had been in Will's exact spot many years ago. He'd had a successful career in finance up until that point, working his way up the corporate ladder and achieving pretty much every goal he set for himself.

"I was around thirty years old at this point, when I was called into my boss's office on a Friday afternoon, where he surprisingly promoted me to a vice president position, making me the youngest ever to achieve that high of a rank. My pay would increase, my team would grow, and of course, I'd have to increase my travel to the other offices," he said. "I'd be part of the executive team, which was incredibly exciting.

"That night, we got a babysitter for our young son, and I took my wife out for dinner to surprise her with the news. It was a fancy restaurant, loud and bustling with people, tons of energy, and I was eager to tell her about the promotion. But I could tell something was bothering her - she'd been extremely quiet on the drive over, which was not like her - so I asked if she was feeling okay."

He paused for a moment, taking another drink of water and clearing his throat. Will thought he was probably close to hitting his limit of talking, but he selfishly wanted to hear the end of his story. Fortunately, Charles clearly wanted to continue.

"All these years later, I look back on that moment as both the worst moment of my life up until that point and the very best thing that could have ever happened to me. She told me that if things didn't change with my job - if I didn't figure out how to prioritize other things in my life, starting with her and Ryan - she didn't think our marriage would make it."

It turned out, Charles shared, that his wife had been unhappy with their marriage for many years. She had hoped that the birth of their son a few years prior would have been a priority for Charles, and it was, albeit only for a short period. She'd wanted to have this conversation with him for some time but hadn't yet found the courage.

"I was shocked at first, having somehow been oblivious to how I'd been acting and how much time my job had been taking, not to mention the stress it was putting me under. I hadn't been taking care of myself physically, either, and had lost a lot of weight. I was so caught up in the need to 'succeed,'" Charles said, using air quotes, "that I had sacrificed everything else in my life. We continued to talk over the rest of dinner, and by the time we got back home, I had made a decision. I walked into the boss's office that next Monday morning and quit."

Will, who had been leaning forward in the recliner, sat back. "Wow, you really quit? What did your boss say?"

"Well, he certainly wasn't happy," Charles said, taking another quick sip of water. "He even offered me more money and a bigger office, thinking at

first that I was negotiating. What he didn't realize was that not only did I need to quit because I
was sacrificing the other parts of my life, but that
I hadn't been happy in this role or at this company
for quite some time. I told him I'd give him a gener-
ous amount of time, six weeks, to find someone to
replace me. But then I'd be gone."

At that point, Nurse Elizabeth returned and was
surprised to see Will still visiting. "Okay, gentlemen,"
she said, "it's just about time for Charles to get his
beauty nap. I'll give you five more minutes before I
send Will out to get lost in the hallways on his way
back to the parking lot. You did get lost on your way
through the hospital to get here, didn't you?"

"What? Never, never," Will replied, feigning shock.

"Uh-huh," she said, smiling. She held up five fingers and said, "You have exactly five minutes."

After she left, Will looked at Charles and said, "I
know you need your rest, but I have to know what
happened next!"

"Luckily, the company only needed me for about
three weeks. I spent the next six months trying
to figure out what I would do with my life. During
that time, I enjoyed a lot of time with my family, of
course, which was priceless.

"My main goal was to figure out what I wanted to do with my career. I read books on career

advice and talked to a few friends, went on long walks to clear my mind . . . I even tried meditation, which I never got the hang of but led to some nice naps . . . but ultimately, it was meeting with three individuals whom I felt had figured this problem out for themselves that set me on the right course."

"Figured out what?" Will asked, leaning forward in his chair once more.

"Ah, for that, you'll have to come back again. I'll start by telling you what I learned from my friend, Stanley," Charles said. He covered his mouth and took a deep yawn. "Lizzy was right, I'm beat."

"Wait . . . *Lizzy*?!"

"Oh, yeah, she said I could call her that. She didn't say the same to you?"

Will frowned. "No, but I guess I now have a new goal. Okay, I'm out of here. Does Wednesday morning work?"

Charles grinned. "Let me check my calendar . . . yep, I think I can fit you in."

And with that, Will left the end-of-life unit of the hospital. And he did get lost on the way back - damn you, Nurse Elizabeth - but eventually made it to the parking lot. Finding his car, he unlocked the door and got in. He rested his head on the steering wheel.

And sobbed.

STANLEY

"Bet you didn't expect to see me here so early," Will said with a wide smile as Nurse Elizabeth looked up at him from behind her computer monitor.

Each day since his last visit, Will had texted Charles to make sure he was okay (he was) and to see if he needed anything (he didn't). Charles always prided himself on being low maintenance, and he certainly didn't want Will worrying about him. Will knew this and had been eager to get back to the hospital to see how his friend was actually doing.

That eagerness led Will to appear at the nurses' station a full 20 minutes before visiting hours officially started. A fact that Nurse Elizabeth did not seem happy about.

Shaking her head and pointing at the clock on the wall behind Will, she said, "Sorry, honey, but you have to wait until 9 a.m. just like everyone else. I can't have visitors showing up all willy-nilly, thinking they can arrive whenever they want." She went back to typing.

Will looked around, peering down each hallway. "Uh, what visitors? It seems like you and I are the only people even in this hospital right now."

She sighed, paused her typing, and looked up at him over the glasses perched on her nose. Before she could respond, however, he set a tray with three cups of coffee that he had been hiding behind his back on the counter.

"Here's the deal, Nurse Elizabeth. This coffee is from my favorite coffee shop in town, The Steaming Cup," he said. "All three are the new Colombian roast they have going. Because I didn't know what kind of coffee you like, one is black, one has just cream, and one has cream and sugar.

"Now, I've had the coffee they serve in this hospital: it's the worst. It tastes like someone dipped an old rag in a mud puddle and then wrung it out into a coffee pot. So, I know that what I have on this counter is pure gold. You can pick whichever you prefer - I'm guessing you're a cream-and-sugar kinda gal - and in exchange, you'll look the other way while I sneak back to visit my old friend. And it will be our little secret."

She squinted her eyes, considering the proposition. Without taking her eyes off of him, she reached up and took the cream-and-sugar cup. She took a sip, looked back at him again, a small smile forming on her face . . . and slowly turned her chair around so she couldn't see him.

He smiled, grabbed the other two cups, and hurried down the hall to room 7A.

Charles was in good spirits this morning, even more so after Will handed him his coffee. "I gotta say, this hospital really is great, but the coffee - not so much." He took a sip of the coffee (black) and said, "Ahhhh . . . now *that's* a cup of coffee."

After they caught up for a few minutes, Will said, "So, you were going to tell me about someone named Stanley?"

"Oh, right," Charles took another sip of coffee. "Good old Stanley Raff. You'd have liked him, I think. Big personality, and he's an advertising guy like people think you are."

Will laughed. Charles knew that, given Will's background, people thought of him as an "advertising guy," which was fair as he *had* built one of the largest advertising agencies in town. But he saw himself much more as an entrepreneur who just happened to start an advertising agency. Honestly, he didn't even really know all that much about advertising, but he kept that bit to himself.

Charles continued. "I had the chance to work with Stanley back in my finance days. I was never a decision-maker on the marketing side of things, obviously, but I was in key marketing meetings as I was responsible for the budget. Getting to see Stanley pitch big ideas was an experience, let me tell you.

"About a month after I quit my job, I was standing in line at a deli when I noticed Stanley sitting at a table in the corner, reading the paper. After I got my sandwich - probably a reuben, I ate a lot of those back then, this was before I realized the importance of focusing on my health - I walked over to his table and asked if I could join him. I wasn't even sure if he'd remember me, to be honest. He always seemed so passionate about his work, and since that was what I was searching for, I figured why not ask him about it."

Stanley did remember Charles and was thrilled to have company. He even knew that Charles had left his job, having noticed that he wasn't in their most recent meeting. "I always liked it when you were in those meetings," he said, his voice deep and gravelly. "Kept me on my toes. Creative-types like me can come up with all the ideas in the world, but if the client can't pay for them, they're worthless."

As Charles continued his story, Will couldn't help but reflect on how lucky he was to have Charles in his life. How many times had they talked like this over the years: Will struggling with a problem, and Charles sharing stories to help shine a light on a possible solution. His body may have been betraying him, but his mind was still as sharp as ever.

"How old was Stanley at this time?" Will asked.

"He was probably about my age now, actually." Charles then began coughing, and it took him a few minutes to get it under control. After taking a sip of water, he continued.

"Stanley eventually asked me what I was up to, and I told him I was reflecting on my career, that it turned out I hadn't ever really been happy with the work I was doing and was taking some time to figure out what was next," Charles said. "And so I told him that it was fortuitous that I had seen him because he was always someone that I thought was full of passion.

"I remember he kind of laughed and said, 'Ah, so you've finally made it.' Confused, I asked, 'Made it to what?'

"'Made it to your midlife work crisis, of course,' he said. 'What took you so long?'"

It turned out, Charles explained, that Stanley had a similar experience early in his career. Unlike Charles, who wanted to get as far away from finance as possible, Stanley was sure he wanted to stay in the advertising industry. But, he wanted his work in advertising to have meaning. His best idea was to help a few local nonprofits in town with their advertising campaigns. When he saw the results of that work - in one case, a homeless shelter was able to double its annual fundraising, helping hundreds of people to receive shelter - he began to feel a spark of purpose in his work.

"Ever since then . . . and we're talking almost twenty years ago . . . I've made sure that my team is not only providing great services to for-profit companies like your previous employer, but we always have a few small charities we're helping, pro bono of course," he told Charles.

Charles paused to sit more upright in his bed, and Will could tell it was a bit of a struggle. He had lost a decent amount of weight by this point, and Will knew that must be particularly tough for him. Charles had always been the most physically fit person he knew.

"I love that idea," Will said. "It makes me think of the times my agency does pro bono work. The team always feels more energized afterward, and of course, I personally feel good that we were able to help."

Charles nodded. "One thing that Stanley pointed out to me was that when they helped a nonprofit, no matter the size of the effort or the charity itself, he felt like he was doing purposeful work. He said he tried to get other agencies to do the same, but they'd always start by focusing on how big of an impact they could have, and they'd spin up a committee and make plans, and . . . it would never happen."

"Interesting," Will said. "So the fact that they were thinking so big ultimately stalled them from making any progress at all. That's part of my problem, too."

"Bingo." Charles pointed at Will. "It was the first big 'aha' moment on my journey to create more meaningful ways to use my talents. I could start small and work my way up."

Will could tell that Charles's energy was starting to stall, and he asked if he could get him anything.

"No, thanks," Charles said. "But I do think I'm about ready for a rest. I'm sure Lizzy will be in soon to kick you out, anyway. How about you come back on Friday, and I can tell you about the meeting I had after talking with Stanley?"

"That works great," Will said, standing up. He leaned over and gave Charles a hug, allowing him to feel just how frail Charles had become.

He dimmed the lights on the way out and, after shutting the door, saw Nurse Elizabeth standing in the hallway looking down at her notepad, making a note about another patient she had just visited.

"So," Will said, getting her attention, "how's our guy doing in there, really?"

She looked toward the door to 7A. "I'm not a doctor, obviously, but if I had to guess, he might have a few weeks. Maybe more, maybe less. I know he seems pretty alert when you see him, but he will likely sleep for the rest of the day. I think he rallies himself for your visits and gives them everything he has, and it wears him out pretty good. He's a tough old guy."

Will looked at her, concern in his eyes. "Oh, I didn't realize . . . maybe I shouldn't come as much, or . . . "

"Oh, no, please don't change anything up with your visits!" she said, interrupting him. "He looks forward to them more than anything. And half the time I'm with him, he can't stop talking about how much he admires you. Personally, I don't get it," she smiled at Will, "but he certainly sees something special in you."

Will's eyes welled up, but he held back any tears. "After my wife, I think he's the most incredible person I've ever met. I'm going to do my best to soak up as much of him as I can while he's still here." He began walking down the hallway to the exit.

Nurse Elizabeth yelled after him, "And you better not try to fool me again with that coffee trick to get in here early. But if you do, maybe a splash of vanilla?"

Will couldn't help but smile as he pushed through the exit door.

ASHLEY

Will didn't show up early on Friday, instead arriving at the hospice wing right at 9 a.m. (though he did bring Nurse Elizabeth a cup of coffee with cream, sugar, and, yes, a splash of vanilla). He would win that woman over - and earn the privilege to call her Lizzy - if it was the last thing he did.

You might not know Will as well as I do - I mean, how could you? But the guy was driven to succeed . . . at everything. It didn't matter how trivial; if there was another level to achieve or a way to measure success, he was going to pursue it.

Come to think of it, that was part of his problem, wasn't it? Being driven to succeed at things that, let's be honest, weren't very important. It's obvious that Lizzy (yes, I get to call her that) liked Will. He was well aware of this, but it wasn't about that. If someone else earned something, even as simple as getting permission to call someone by their nickname, he'd need to earn that, too.

Will carefully followed the arrows on the floor, successfully locating the pink arrow leading him to the double doors marking the entrance to the hospice wing. Holding his coffee tray, he turned and backed through the doors, hearing a familiar laugh.

And there, chatting with Nurse Elizabeth at the nurses' station, was his good friend Shera. And they were . . . giggling?!

Will and Shera go way back, having first met when he was a consultant (at a company called Ideathon . . . really, who comes up with these names?), and she having recently started her software company, Friendly People. Charles had introduced them, in fact.

I should point out that if you end up liking Shera (which is a mixed bag; she's not for everyone) then you might consider checking out The Great Team Turnaround *and* The Purpose Playbook. *They're chock full of Shera-ness.*

Shera noticed Will and ran toward him, arms wide, almost jumping into his arms. She was a hugger, always had been, but Will could feel something more in this hug. They each looked up to Charles - he was a mentor, investor, and friend to both of them - and this was the first time they'd seen each other since Charles got sick.

They walked over to the nurses' station, and Shera said, "Lizzy here was just telling me about the time she . . . "

Will didn't hear anything else Shera said, because . . . Lizzy?! Already? Maybe she had come earlier in the week and had met Nurse Elizabeth already.

"I didn't realize," Will said, interrupting whatever Shera had been talking about, "that you had already visited Charles in this wing, Shera."

She shook her head. "No, this is the first time. I did visit Charles a few months back. I'm sorry I missed you then. But what I was saying - Lizzy and I both just realized . . . "

Once again tuning out Shera's story - the last thing he wanted to hear about right now was some funny experience they shared between them - he scanned the desk and saw a big bouquet of flowers with a card that said "Charles" on it. So, that was for Charles, but what gift had she brought for Nurse Elizabeth that had immediately bonded the two of them?

No, it appeared she just came in being all . . . her . . . and had won Nurse Elizabeth over in a matter of minutes. Outrageous!

I told you Will had a problem.

Will tuned back into Shera's story, quickly picking up the thread (apparently, Shera and Lizzy had the same kind of dog, whoopidee doo). When she finished he said, "Okay, shall we go see the big guy?"

"Sure, let's go," Shera said. Will pulled Nurse Elizabeth's coffee out of the drink tray that The Steaming Cup had given him and handed it to her.

"For me?" She said, a big grin on her face. "Oh, Will, you shouldn't have . . . but I'm glad you did." She gave him a wink, and he decided to take that as a win.

As they walked down the hall toward Charles's room, Shera held the flowers in one arm and wrapped her other arm around Will's. She asked,

"I'm a little nervous. I've been a bit of a mess ever since you texted me that Charles had been moved to hospice. How's he looking?"

"Well," Will said as they paused in front of the door to 7A, "your best friend back there told me that he saves up his stamina for these visits, and then just about collapses afterward. He looks much weaker and coughs a good deal more than he did before, but overall, he seems to be in pretty good spirits."

"Okay, ready?" He asked. She nodded, so he knocked on the door, and Charles yelled for them to come in.

Shera immediately rushed up to hug Charles, who was sitting up in his bed with a crossword puzzle book in his lap. Will made his way over to the bed, and, realizing Shera might never let go, gently pulled on her shoulders, saying, "Okay, okay, I'm pretty sure being able to breathe is a critical part of Charles's care."

She stepped back, allowing Will to go in for his hug.

"Uh, Charles," she said, gesturing at her flowers. "Where in the world should I put *these*? It looks like the botanical gardens set up a pop-up exhibit in here!"

Indeed, flowers were covering just about every flat surface in the room.

"Yes, I know. It's quite embarrassing. I think someone let the word out that I was in here." He looked at Will, who shook his head that it wasn't him.

It totally was.

While Shera looked for a spot to put her flowers, Will grabbed a second chair, pulled it over next to Charles's bed and sat down. Shera came over and sat beside him, and they both looked up at their hero.

"It's so good to see you two," he said. Then, looking at Shera, he asked, "Tell me how you're doing. How's the company doing? And what's the latest with Fletch?"

Fletch was the name of Shera's dog (or rather, Irwin F. Fletcher, if we're being specific), a name that both Charles and Will had suggested. Shera had never seen the movie - and never planned to, mind you - but she oddly thought her dog kind of did look like a "Fletch," so she went with it. And since you're now a fan of the film, having watched it recently, I'm sure you'll agree it's a fine name for a dog.

After she caught them both up on how things were going (business was great, and Fletch was doing well but still barking too much at other dogs on their walks), Will asked about Megan.

Megan, a central character in The Great Team Turnaround, *is one of Shera's top leaders at Friendly People.*

"Oh, you know Megan, she's terrific and crushing everything I give her, as usual. In fact, she doesn't know it, but I'm prepping her to run the company eventually. In a few years, I intend to take a less active role, probably rolling into the Board Chair position, and I think she's just the person to step in as CEO," she said. "Kind of like you did with Rachel, Will."

"The best decision I ever made. And I think Megan will be a great CEO when the time is right," Will said. "How's Rosie doing?"

Remember that talking robot I mentioned earlier? Well, that's Rosie the Robot, the Friendly People receptionist. She's a major figure in The Great Team Turnaround, *and Will had to work hard to win her over (much the same way he's currently trying to win over Nurse Elizabeth, now that I think about it).*

He really does have issues, doesn't he?

Shera smiled. "She's great. Still asks about you, though sometimes she pretends not to know your name and asks, 'Where's that guy with the bad dad jokes?'"

They all laughed, which prompted Charles to start coughing. Shera gave Will a concerned look, and he mouthed, 'It's okay.' Will handed him his water, and after he stopped coughing, he took a small sip.

"Sorry, that tends to happen when I laugh. I think this guy has been doing it on purpose," he nodded to Will with a grin. "Shera, I'm really glad you came today. I was going to share a story with Will to help him with his problem, and I think you'll appreciate it as well."

Shera looked at Will and asked, "Your … *problem*?"

Will then filled Shera in on his inability to find meaning in his work as he reflected back on his career. He explained that Charles was sharing stories from his past, bringing her up to speed on Stanley Raff's ability to find meaning in his work by using his team to help local nonprofits. "And today," Will said, "he is going to tell me - us - about someone else he met. That right, Charles?"

"That's right, Will." Charles looked at Shera. "I had quit my job and was on a quest to figure out what I wanted to do. I didn't have any real clue what that might be other than I knew I wanted to be in-spired and for my work to have meaning. Stanley helped me see that one option would be to use my workplace to help others. And it had obviously worked for him.

"At the end of our meeting in the deli, Stanley suggested that I meet up with his wedding pho-tographer," Charles said, pausing to take another sip of water.

Will and Shera looked at each other, and Shera asked, "His wedding photographer?"

"That's right, I was equally puzzled. But he just said, 'Trust me, she's the perfect person for you to meet,' and gave me her information. I walked straight across the parking lot of the deli and called her from the payphone.

"Don't give me that look, you two; I know you both know what a payphone is," he said, seeing their feigned looks of confusion.

"Oh, right," Shera said. "Where Superman changes into his costume."

"It's not a *costume*," Will said, "and in fact, many people argue that what he wears when he's Superman are his *actual* clothes, whereas what he wears when he's Clark Kent is . . . "

"Uh, children," Charles said, waving his hands in the air. "How about you discuss the details of

Superman's wardrobe choices later? I've got a story to tell and not a lot of time to tell it. Lizzy is liable to bound in here and kick you out before I even get to the good part."

They acquiesced, though Will gave Shera a this-is-definitely-not-over look. "Sorry, Charles, please continue."

"Her name was Ashley. As she put it, any friend of Stanley's was a friend of hers and offered to meet up. She suggested meeting at the end of the following week for coffee or joining her on one of her photo shoots earlier in the week. Eager to continue making progress, I chose the shoot."

He paused and looked at the clock on the wall. "You know what, it's actually time for my exercise. I'm kind of surprised Lizzy hasn't . . . " Just then, the door to his room opened, and Lizzy entered. She said, "Okay, Charles, it's time for your morning walk. Shera and Will, you're welcome to take him if you like; he knows the route."

She gestured to a walker. "This is your standard walker. It's there mostly to help Charles with stability, just in case. Now, he's going to tell you he doesn't need to use it . . . "

"I don't!" Charles said, interrupting her. "The damn thing makes me look like I'm 100 years old!"

" . . . but you need to assure me that you'll make him use it," she said, not paying attention to him. "Otherwise, I'll have to take over, and you two will have to wait here. So, what's it going to be? Are you two up for this?"

They assured her that they were. Charles began to shuffle his way out of bed, and Shera and Will stood on each side of him so he could use them for stability. Charles put an arm around each of their necks and lowered himself to the floor.

Lizzy brought over his walker. He glowered at her but begrudgingly grabbed it with both hands and said, "Okay, let's do this if we must."

"Don't let him fool you," Nurse Elizabeth said, "his walks are one of his favorite parts of the day. Word around here is that he used to be some kind of athlete or something."

Charles grumbled, but he had a smile on his face nonetheless. They led him into the hallway, and after a few minutes, Will noticed that he needed the walker more than he let on.

"I arrived at the address she gave me expecting some kind of wedding venue," Charles said, jumping back into the story, "but instead, it was a small house in a modest neighborhood on the outskirts of town.

"I knocked on the door, and a woman answered. I asked if she was Ashley, as I wasn't able to look her up because this was before the Internet. She told me no, her name was Diane Parker, and offered for me to come in as Ashley was just getting set up."

Charles motioned for them to take the left hallway, continuing the story. Ashley had been in the living room, positioning her camera and lighting equipment in front of a fireplace. "Oh, great, I'm glad you made it, Charles," she said, shaking his hand. "The family should be in any minute."

Confused, Charles asked if these were pre-wedding photos, and Ashley looked at him, equally confused. "Wait, did Stanley not tell you what I do outside of wedding photography?"

"No, he sure didn't," Charles replied.

"Oh, wow. Well, this will be very different from what you were expecting," she said. "When I'm not shooting weddings, I spend my free time taking photos of families with a terminally ill loved one."

Just then, Diane came in, asking if Ashley was ready. She indicated she was, so Diane said she'd be right back.

"So, wait," Charles said, "Diane has a family member who's . . . "

"Her husband has been given a few weeks to live, yes," she said. "And I'll be photographing the two of them and their two children, and since you're here, you can help."

Two hours later, Ashley and Charles were sitting at a restaurant near the Parkers' home. Charles had insisted that she let him buy her lunch after what he had just witnessed.

After ordering their meals, Charles said, "That was such a . . . moving . . . experience, Ashley. I'm surprised Stanley didn't tell me what you do."

"Why did he say you should meet with me?" She asked.

Charles informed her of the journey he was on, finding meaning in his work, and that Stanley had said Ashley would be the perfect person for him to meet up with.

"And now that I see what you do outside of your 'day job,' I think I get it. See, Stanley had found a way to make the work he does more meaningful, using his team to help charities in town. Whereas it seems like you're using your photography *skills* to help people outside of the work you do," he said.

Nodding, Ashley said, "That makes sense. Being a wedding photographer has its own benefits, as you get to see people on one of the best days of their lives. You should have seen Stanley's wedding . . ." she laughed. "Actually, I did all *three* of his weddings. Each of them more opulent than the last and very fun to shoot."

"How did you end up taking photos of, well . . ." Charles stumbled on the words, not sure what to say.

"Of people who are dying?" She asked. "Well, unlike Stanley, who I know was looking for a way to find more meaning in his work, I was pretty content with what I was doing. Yes, it was hard work, and most of it wasn't very glamorous, but it was still meaningful to me."

She then explained that one of her family members had been diagnosed with a terminal illness and that a friend had come to photograph them before her loved one passed away. The impact of having those photographs, as well as the thoughtfulness of someone helping in that way, inspired her to do the same for others.

"Ever since then, I've been trying to help people experiencing loss and grief by using my skills in photography to help. The Parkers are the third family I've shot this week," she said as their food arrived.

As they ate, Charles began to see why Stanley had wanted him to talk with Ashley. She beamed as she talked about the work she did, and not only the work helping families going through loss. It was apparent that having that outlet to use her skills to help others actually infused more meaning in her 'day job.'

"And that," Charles said to Shera and Will, "was the second experience that began shaping how I would eventually find meaning in my work and career." They had made a few loops around the hospital wing, and were nearing room 7A. "I think," he said, pausing to catch his breath, "perhaps it's time for me to rest."

They walked back into his room and helped him into his bed, his body weak as they supported him. Once he was situated, with a few pillows behind his back, he said, "You know, it wasn't that long ago that I did the Cradle Ride in South Africa, and now I can barely walk around this hospital floor for a half hour. Funny how life works, isn't it?"

Will and Shera only nodded, not thinking it was funny in the slightest. They knew about his many adventures cycling, climbing, or running all over the globe. He was once the fittest person they knew, often making them exercise with him during their mentoring sessions. And they knew it was extremely hard for him to deal with his current physical condition. What they did not know was what to say in that moment.

Sensing this, Charles said, "Hey, you two, don't look like that! I know what's coming, and I'm good with it. I feel like I've led a purposeful life, at least for the last thirty years or so, and I'm at peace moving onto . . . well, whatever comes next. And you two listening to me babble on about one aspect of that purposeful life - being inspired by my work - is just what the doctor ordered. Well . . . not literally."

They all laughed at that, releasing some tension from the room. The laughing did lead to another coughing fit by Charles, but this time, it felt worth it. Shera asked, "So, Charles, I'm curious what ever happened with Ashley's work helping others. Did she keep it going? Is she still pursuing it?"

Charles smiled. "To my knowledge, she's still doing it, yes. Perhaps the most amazing part of her story is that, over time, a few people she provided her service to were also photographers. Some of those photographers asked how they could help, seeking a way to give back and support others the way Ashley had helped them. A movement began to grow very organically. The last time I checked, there were several hundred photographers around the country, and several in other parts of the world, photographing families as they face a terminal illness."

Ashley's story, and indeed the work she does to photograph families with a terminally ill family member, is not-so-loosely based on the incredibly inspiring Ashley Jones, founder and CEO of Momento Foundation. She has a powerful book, When You Can't See the Light, *which she describes as a 'trauma-informed guide to surviving significant loss.' I've found it makes a wonderful gift for people who are struggling with grief.*

"Wow, that's incredible," Will said. "All that growth happened because Ashley had an instinct to pay forward the gift that someone had given her during a time of need."

"That's right," Charles said, "and similar to Stanley's story, I don't know that someone could have started with the goal of inspiring hundreds of people to provide that service. It started with a small concept, which was enough for Ashley. That small, singular instinct set in motion a much larger movement.

"Okay, friends," he said, "I'm wiped. Thank you so much for hanging out with me today. You make this old man very proud."

They hugged their goodbyes and turned down the lights as they left his room. As they passed the nurses' station, Nurse Elizabeth motioned Will to come over, indicating that she wanted to share something with him. Shera got the hint and stayed back, pulling out her phone to respond to a few messages.

"Will, I think you might want to come back sooner than later. Charles's most recent test results . . . weren't very promising. I don't think we're talking *days* . . . but he might only have a week or so left. His body is starting to break down at an accelerated rate. I'm sorry, I just thought you should know."

Will thanked her and walked over to Shera, who put her phone back in her purse as he approached. She saw the look on Will's face. "It's not good news, is it?"

He opened his mouth to say something, but the words wouldn't come out, so he just shook his head. Together, they walked toward the exit.

NICK

Over the weekend, Will checked in on Charles a few times over text. The news that Charles's latest test results were worse than expected had really shaken him. Charles assured him he was doing fine, but Will was eager to get back to him on Monday morning nonetheless.

He had reached out to Rachel, the president of his agency, to let her know about Charles' situation. She asked if she could go with him to visit on Monday, and he readily accepted. They had a big brother-little sister type of relationship, and while she didn't know Charles as well as Will did, she very much cared for him. And, Will assumed correctly, she probably wanted to be there to support them both.

They arrived at the hospital at 8:55 a.m., parking a few spots over from one another. After helping her negotiate the old-school parking meter, Will led her into the hospital, and they began following the green arrow.

"So this nurse . . . what was her name again?" Rachel asked.

"Nurse Elizabeth. To me, at least," Will said as they made the correct turn onto the pink-arrowed path.

"Right, Nurse Elizabeth. You said she likes you; I mean, how could she not, am I right?" She said, softly elbowing him in the ribs. "And you're all bent out of shape because she hasn't suggested that you call her Lizzy?"

Yes, Will had been telling Rachel all about the 'Lizzy situation.' Like me, she knew Will pretty well and was only mildly surprised he'd found himself in this . . . predicament. If you could even call it that.

"I know, I know," he said, shaking his head. "It's silly, but I've tried everything short of giving her a friendship bracelet! I even keep bringing her coffee, just the way she likes it, and nothing."

Rachel looked at the tray in his hands - four cups this time, including Rachel's preferred herbal blueberry green tea - and noticed the little to-go bag he was holding. "And, I presume, one of The Steaming Cup's famous cinnamon danishes?"

He shrugged. "I have to try *something*."

She laughed as they pushed their way through the double doors of the hospice unit. The nurses' station was empty, so Will put Nurse Elizabeth's coffee and danish on the counter. He found a piece of paper, then wrote, 'For Nurse Elizabeth, from Will.'

They made their way down the hall and, upon entering Charles's room, found him over by the window sitting in a wheelchair. His face lit up. "Oh, Rachel, thank you so much for coming. It's so good to see you!"

Rachel hugged him and asked how he was doing.

"You know, not so great. Lizzy stuck me in this wheelchair over the weekend, saying something about me not being stable enough to walk on my own," looking down at his legs. "I guess she's right; I fell down on Saturday morning when I got out of bed. Perhaps laying down all day and being pumped full of medicine does a number on one's strength."

Will noticed the full plate of food on the bedside table. "Not hungry this morning, Charles?"

"Oh, I'll eat, stop your worrying. You two bring a chair over here and join me by this sunlight . . . and bring an extra chair with you," Charles said, turning his face toward the large window. "I want to soak up this sunlight. It feels like ages since I felt the sun on my skin."

They grabbed the chairs and approached the window, Rachel sitting to his right and Will to his left. Will set the extra chair next to him. "Someone joining us today?"

"I've asked your book publisher to stop by. I think he'll be able to shine some light on the conversation we've been having," Charles said.

"Nick?" Will asked.

"That's right. The one and only Nick Andrews," Charles replied. He looked at Rachel and said, "Nick and I go way back, and I introduced him to Will when he was thinking about writing his first book."

"I think I met Nick at your book launch event, didn't I?" Rachel asked, looking at Will.

Will nodded. "Yep, really nice guy. I'm just not sure how he'll be able to help."

"Trust me on this one, Will. Nick helped me nail what I think is the most important aspect of finding purpose in your work," he said. Noticing the confused look on Rachel's face, he added, "Will, why don't you fill Rachel in on what we've been talking about."

Will began explaining to Rachel that he'd been feeling like his career carried little purpose in the world. Rachel interjected, suggesting that he'd made a huge impact on many people's lives, including hers.

"I appreciate that, I do," he said. "And I don't discount it, but that's not why I built the company, or at least it wasn't the main reason. I just want to feel more inspired by the work I choose to do, and maybe feel like I'm making an impact beyond simply helping me and my family."

"And you think," she said, turning to Charles, "that Nick might be able to help him?"

"Help him with what?"

They turned and saw Nick in the doorway of Charles's room. He had a single flower in a vase in one hand and a blue envelope in the other. He was dressed in a suit, satchel bag slung over his shoulder, and had a big smile on his face. Every time Will had seen him, he'd been smiling.

"Nick, my old friend, come on in here! I'd get up and hug you, but, well . . . " Charles gestured down at his legs.

"You stay right there, Charles," Nick said, "but first, let me figure out where I should put this flower . . . " Turning toward Will and Rachel, he added, "Charles told me the place was overflowing with vegetation, and I can see that he was right, so he begged me not to bring any more. I couldn't help it, though, and plucked this beauty from my garden on the way over." He looked around and found what appeared to be the last available counter spot to set the vase.

After greeting everyone, he sat down in the chair next to Will. "So, what were you all talking about?"

Charles filled him in on their conversation, and Will couldn't help but notice how raspy and weak his voice sounded. At least he hadn't had a coughing fit yet. But still, he didn't sound good.

When Charles finished, Nick said, "Ah, I take it you want me to tell the story of how I started my book publishing company?"

Charles nodded, and, never one to shy away from telling a story, Nick jumped in.

"I got a degree in writing and journalism and quickly found myself working at a small-town newspaper. It was pretty thankless work, even back then, and after a handful of years, I was already feeling burnt out. I took a few contracting jobs - writing columns for a few magazines, even producing content for a couple of advertising agencies - but it wasn't until I got a ghostwriting job that I figured out what I was meant to be doing.

"I had agreed to help a young woman with her book without even knowing what the book was about. At that point, I just needed a new contract, so I would have taken almost any job. I guess the man upstairs was looking out for me because it was this random job that taught me so much."

He explained that he met the author in a local park to learn about her project and talk through his process of ghostwriting. She didn't have a title for her book yet - oftentimes, book titles solidify as the book starts to come together - but she knew what she wanted to write. She explained to him that she was biracial, having a Black father and a white mother. And how, as a biracial child, she was, for the most part, seen as 'different' by her peers, not feeling like she ever truly fit in.

"She told me that she was four months pregnant with her first child, a little girl. It was critically important that her daughter feel comfortable and confident in her skin. Her book would help biracial children feel a sense of belonging and acceptance, knowing they weren't alone."

Then, gesturing at himself, said, "And you can probably tell from looking at me that I didn't have a lot of experience with that topic, and I told her that, in case she wanted to find another writing partner. But for whatever reason, she decided to stick with me, and we immediately got to work. I later found out that she was self-funding the book, as no publishing company had accepted her proposal.

"Now that I'm in the industry, I can see why. It's a very insular business in which who you know is more important than the story you're trying to tell. And if you don't have any connections or you're not already a well-known person, you can pretty much forget about getting picked up," he sighed. "And there are so many important stories that need to be told, just like this one!"

He shared that the author wanted to include interviews with other biracial adults discussing their childhood experiences and what they thought helped them along their journeys. "The stories I heard while doing those interviews, well . . . they just broke my heart. These people were experiencing things I didn't even know were part of the human experience! I knew about racism, of course, but was unaware that biracial children and adults are often caught in between, receiving the worst treatment from both sides."

He paused momentarily, looking at each of them. "As I said, my heart was broken, and I became determined to make sure I gave everything I had to make this book as good as possible. Ultimately, we created two versions of the book: a children's book, and a more educational book for adults."

"Amazing," Will said. "I saw that book on your website when Charles first introduced us, and I can't wait to order a copy now!"

"No need," Nick said, reaching into his bag. "I bring copies with me everywhere I go." He then handed Rachel and Will a copy of the adult version.

"I've seen the power of kids and adults alike reading this book. If even just one child reads this and feels like they have a place of belonging in this world, that's enough for me. That child may grow up to be happier and positively affect those around them. Those unseen ripple effects are what I believe will make the world the place we want it to be."

There was silence in the room for a few minutes as they all absorbed what Nick had just said.

"Well, now it's pretty obvious how you came up with the name of your publishing company," Will said. "I'm curious if the success of that book helped you fund your business."

"Actually, I *lost* money on that project. Might have something to do with the fact that I waived my fees," Nick chuckled. "I got so swept up in the impact that I believed the book would make, and I knew that the author was pulling everything from her savings to make it happen that I simply couldn't send her a bill. She kept asking me when I would send the first invoice, and I would always tell her it was 'in the mail.' In fact, that's still a running joke between us all these years later."

"Okay, now I have to ask why you took on *my* book project. I don't think it's nearly as important as a book like that," Will said. "I can't see how it's important beyond maybe helping a few CMOs act more entrepreneurial."

"Are you kidding?" Nick said. "Will, your book helps people think like an entrepreneur! It gives them a blueprint to change the course of their career, if not their life."

They're talking about Will's book, The 5-Day Turnaround, *which does indeed help people with those things and, yes, has the same name as the TLU book in which we first meet Will. As far as the name of the publishing company,*

*well, you can check the back cover of this book
to guess what that might be. (Look, you're
allowed to steal ideas from yourself).*

"I guess so, but I never really thought of it like
that," Will said.

"Will," Rachel said, "I've met so many people
who said your book helped them get out of a jam at
their job or who ended up starting their own company because your words gave them the confidence
to take the leap. And you know Matt will forever be
grateful for the help you gave him, which inspired
your book in the first place."

*Matt is one of the main characters in the TLU,
and he was also first introduced in the book* The
5-Day Turnaround. *The real one.*

Charles smiled as he watched the revelation on
Will's face that maybe he'd been making a difference with his work all along, even if he hadn't been
aware of it.

"So, Nick," Charles said, leading the witness,
"would you say that in finding meaning in your
work, you embraced the idea that small ideas can
lead to a bigger impact and that focusing on doing
purposeful work, no matter how insignificant it

may seem, can lead to . . . " A sudden, violent cough-ing fit hit Charles at that moment, and Will asked if he should call Nurse Elizabeth in.

"No, it's okay, Will, but thanks. I'm alright . . . " Charles said between coughs, almost whispering as his voice was really fading now. "Nick, please continue my thought as I'm sure you know where I was going."

Once the coughing subsided, Nick continued with Charles's thought: "Right you are, Charles. No matter how small meaningful work may seem, getting started on it is the key. At a minimum, you'll feel good about yourself. And there's always a chance that your efforts will have a ripple effect beyond anything you could imagine."

"One of the things Charles helped me realize was that, as I have been trying to figure out a way to create more purpose to my work," Will said, "I had this feeling that whatever I chose to do needed to have a really big impact . . . and the pressure of that scale was stopping me from getting started."

"It really is just like your book, Will," Rachel said. "Not that it was a small feat - I know how hard you worked on writing it and getting it out into the world - but that one effort has made a pretty siz-able impact on other people's lives."

Nick smiled (or rather, kept smiling) and added, "I think the key for you, Will, is to appreciate the fact that whatever you do next, you need to make sure you are purposeful about the impact you hope to have, and that you start by dreaming small. Knowing that no matter what, you'll feel good about your effort, and it's a bonus if it grows into something larger. Give those ripple effects a chance to get going."

And with that, Nick announced that he had to leave, prompting Will and Rachel to do the same. It was pretty clear that Charles was worn out, and while Will did appreciate that these visits were helping Charles in some way, they were also quite demanding on him physically.

"I'll be back tomorrow at 9 a.m. sharp," Will said to Charles as he leaned over and gave him a big hug. Then, smiling, he added: "Make sure to eat your breakfast before I arrive. I have an idea, and you'll need your strength . . . "

THE WALK

"Knock, knock, anyone home?" Will asked through the crack in Charles's hospital room door. Once again, he had arrived at the appropriate time for visitors, and once again, he had a tray of coffee in his hand.

He heard Nurse Elizabeth call from inside the room, "Come on in." He entered and saw only her in the room, making Charles's bed. Noticing the look of semi-panic on Will's face, she said, "Oh, good morning, honey. Charles is in the bathroom, no need to worry."

Will released a literal sigh of relief and handed her a coffee, which she happily accepted.

"I didn't get to say thank you yesterday for the danish. It was delicious," she said, sipping her coffee. "This coffee is *so* good! Thank you!"

"No problem, and sorry, they were out of danishes this morning," he said. He looked around the room and noticed the crossword puzzle book in the trash can by Charles's bed. He gestured toward it and said, "Well, that's a good sign, right? To finish an entire crossword puzzle book?"

Nurse Elizabeth frowned and stepped closer to him. She lowered her voice, presumably so Charles wouldn't hear from the bathroom. "No, Will, he got too frustrated with it earlier this morning and threw it in the trash. He said he couldn't concentrate long enough to get any of the answers out of his head."

They heard a flush from the bathroom, and a few minutes later, Charles knocked on the door. Nurse Elizabeth opened it, helping him negotiate his wheelchair out of the bathroom.

"Will!" he said, with a little too much energy as it led to a small coughing fit.

"Take it easy, Charles," Nurse Elizabeth said. "If you get too excited too soon, I'll have to kick this young man out sooner than he wants so you can rest." She positioned him over by the bed and said,

"Okay, you two have fun. I'm going on a short break and I'll check in on you a bit later."

As she left, Will went in for his hug and then moved Charles over toward the door. He peeked out into the hallway and, seeing that it was empty, turned to Charles and said, "Okay, the coast is clear. You ready for a little adventure?"

Not knowing what was in store but dying to have some kind of break in the monotony, Charles said with a big grin, "Boy, am I ever!"

Will wheeled Charles out of the room and silently closed it behind them. He put a finger to his mouth, motioning for Charles to keep quiet, and began pushing him down the hallway. Following the arrows, this time pink to green, he took Charles down to the lobby . . . and right out the front door.

Thirty minutes later, they entered Foothills Park. Will had positioned them on a bench in front of the skatepark, having helped Charles out of his wheelchair in the hopes that he'd feel more like himself. It worked, as he hadn't seen Charles this rejuvenated since he first entered the hospital.

"Lizzy is going to kill you," he said with a huge grin. "I'm going to tell her that you kidnapped me because otherwise, she'll kill me, too." They both laughed at that, and Will agreed that a kidnapping was the best way to represent their journey to the park. No sense for Charles to be collateral damage.

They sat there for a few minutes, watching people skateboard up and down the many ramps and bowls, some successfully pulling off a great feat of acrobatics, others not so much, but everyone having fun. It was a beautiful day.

"So, what did you learn from my story, Will?" Charles asked.

Will smiled at the question. Charles was a great mentor. In Will's opinion, part of the reason Charles was so effective was his ability to help you find your path forward through sharing his own experiences, letting you realize the solution on your own. And he'd asked this question many times before, so Will was ready to respond.

"I think I've got it," Will said. "First, you shared Stanley's story, which showed me that I could use the current work I do to help others. Next, you shared Ashley's story, which helped me see that I could continue with what I'm doing but use my skills to help others. And then you had Nick visit us in the hospital, and he completely re-oriented his career to focus entirely on helping others."

Charles nodded, encouraging him to go on. "As I think about wanting to find meaning in my work, that gives me three possible directions: use my current job, do work outside my job, or change my job entirely. In all these cases, using my skills to do good will help me lead a more meaningful and purpose-driven life."

"Nicely done. But what do all of those stories have in common?" Charles asked. "What's the through-line that weaves them together?"

Will thought about this for a minute, then said, "The key, it appears, is to start by dreaming small. In each of their cases, they began by doing something that, in the grand scheme of things, might be considered insignificant. However, with each of those small starts they found their way, in some cases allowing the ripple effects to have a bigger impact, and in some, simply allowing the effects to help them derive more meaning in their own lives."

"You got it," Charles said. "And don't forget about the fourth example, which I think brings the point home perfectly."

Will looked at Charles with a puzzled expression. "I thought you only told three stories . . ."

"I did, but remember, this all started with us having a chance encounter with The Skateman at this very park. He perhaps embodies the concept of dreaming small better than anyone, happy to simply try to make one person smile each day. For him, that's enough," Charles said.

They sat for a few more minutes before Will, checking his watch, decided they had better start their walk back. "I can handle Nurse Elizabeth wanting to kill me, but if she calls the cops on us, that'd be bad."

Will helped Charles into his wheelchair and began pushing him, taking the long way through the park to give them a few extra, precious minutes.

As they exited the park entrance and began traveling on the sidewalk toward the hospital, Charles said, "After figuring out the key to building a meaningful career - by using my skills to do good and beginning by dreaming small - I got to work. This is when I first developed the PVTV methodology."

PVTV, or Purpose, Vision, Tenets, & Values, is the construct used in the other TLU books. The Purpose Playbook, officially Book Five in the series, dives deep into the process - if you are interested.

Charles paused every few sentences, allowing himself to catch his breath. "Remember, I created the PVTV for a company that I wanted to start ... without even knowing the industry! I knew that if I was pointed toward the purpose I had developed for myself - to have an outsized, positive impact on the world - no matter what kind of business I started, I'd be moving in the right direction.

"In fact, that purpose and new direction for my life led me to help develop the park we were just in. Knowing that I was helping others have a safe place to exercise and get fresh air in a thriving city was something that I knew would have that ripple effect that Nick was talking about."

They were approaching the hospital now, and Will began to walk a little slower. "Charles . . . listen . . . I just want you to know . . . "

Charles reached back and put his hand on Will's hand, patting it.

"I know, Will. I know."

CHARLES

Three days later, Will pulled into the parking lot of Silver Cross Hospital. It was beginning to mist outside - the forecast called for storms later in the day - so he grabbed his umbrella out of the trunk. He carefully set the coffee tray on the roof of his car, threw some money in the parking meter, and hopped up onto the sidewalk, avoiding a puddle at the last minute.

He saw Nurse Elizabeth in front of Charles's door, writing something on her clipboard, and said hello. Before she could respond, he realized his hands were empty and said, "Oh, shoot, I forgot the coffee. Be right back."

As he started to turn, she grabbed his arm to stop him. He looked at her and noticed that her eyes were red and swollen. He turned and pushed open the door to Charles's room, seeing it was empty. The bed was made, and all the flowers were gone.

"When?" He asked, turning back to her.

"Late last night, around midnight. He left you this card. I'm so sorry, Will, I really am," she said.

Will took the card and looked back into the room, his eyes welling up. The two of them stood there next to each other until Will was able to choke out a few words.

"You were so great to him, Nurse Elizabeth. I'll never forget how you cared for him in his final weeks."

"Thank you, Will." Then, putting her arm around him, she added, "But please, don't call me Nurse Elizabeth. My real friends call me Liz."

EPILOGUE

The loss of Charles hit Will pretty hard, as one could expect. With Will's permission, Charles named him the executor of his estate. Everything had been in order. "Don't worry, I'm not going to leave you with some huge mess; I just need someone to sign a few papers and make sure a few checks get to the right place," Charles had said, and Will actually found the process helped him deal with his grief. He hadn't been ready for Charles to leave, and spending time at his home, making sure everything was the way he had wanted it, let him spend a little more time with his mentor and friend.

At the funeral, Will gave the eulogy, which he found surprisingly cathartic. Sarah helped out with the arrangements, and Danni read a poem. The whole gang was there, including Liz, whom Will had made a point to keep in contact with, bringing her coffee, with cream, sugar, and a dash of vanilla, every week or so. And every once in a while, one of those famous danishes.

We now find Will, six months later, at the cemetery, standing on a hill in front of three gravestones. His bike rests on the newly installed bike stand just down the hill. Charles had complained to Will many times that there weren't enough bike stands in the city and had pledged to do something about it. Now, thanks to Charles, there were twenty-five new bike stands in various places around town. In his will, there was a stipulation that "Under no circumstances whatsoever should my name be placed on the bike stands. I'm doing this to help, not to boost my legacy, of all things."

Even from the grave, Charles remained a staunch opponent of legacy-chasing.

W ill carefully pulled three flowers from his backpack, putting one in front of each gravestone. Charles had secured a spot in the cemetery beside his wife and son.

"Sorry I haven't been here in a few weeks," Will said. Gesturing down the hill toward the bike stand, he added, "But, you'll be happy to know that I got your bike tuned up . . . sorry, *my* bike . . . you know darn well it's way more complex than anything I deserve to be riding! That bike is like a magnet for serious cyclists. They come up to me all the time asking about it and are generally aghast that I have no clue what they are talking about. Anyway, I've started riding it more. I've decided that from now on, unless the weather is too bad, I'm going to ride it here to visit you. I figured you'd like that."

He walked up to Charles's gravestone and brushed some dirt off it. Then, as he usually did, he sat on the ground next to it as if they were sitting together. "You sure did pick a great spot, my friend," he said. "This view is spectacular. You can just about see the entire city from up here.

"Foothills Park has finally started building the rock climbing addition you donated. As you probably expected, I had to get involved on the committee to ensure it moved forward and didn't get stuck in what you call 'death by committee.' They were definitely headed in that direction. I worked them through creating their PVTV, and once that was locked down, everything started to flow nicely. It will likely be a year until it launches, but everyone is excited about it.

"Speaking of PVTV, I've made a big decision. I'm going to try to help more companies develop and run the PVTV methodology. I've had so much success with it at the agency, as well as helping a few clients like Titan and SalesLive, that I think it's time to see how many more teams it can help. And to your point about dreaming small, I will take it one company at a time. Maybe there will be some ripple effects from it. But I know one thing: the world could use more purpose-driven companies and teams."

Smiling, Will said, "Oh, you'll love this. Danni took an entrepreneurship class! I was so excited when she told me that I even offered to speak at one of their classes, an idea she said would cause her to 'drop out of school and become a hermit out of embarrassment.' Unfortunately . . . she was bored to tears and barely skated by with a B. Oh well, you can't win 'em all.

"She's already planning the month-long trip you gave her as a graduation present, even though it's still over two years away. I know that Loch Ness and Edinburgh are on the itinerary. Ever since you told her about that trip, she's always wanted to go."

Will sometimes acted like Charles was talking back to him, imagining what he might say. It comforted him to believe that he was an active participant in their conversation.

"What? No, Sarah and I won't try to meet up with her during the trip, don't be silly." Then, with a sly grin, he added, "But if we just happen to be on our own trip and by pure circumstance happen to bump into her … well, I'm just saying anything can happen."

He picked up a long piece of grass and began twisting it around his fingers. He could see clouds out in the distance, casting a long shadow over part of the town.

"I've got another thing I'm working on. Rachel and I have kicked around an idea for a few years but were always stymied by the large scope of trying to pull it off. But, putting our 'dream small' hats on, I think we've come up with a way to get started."

Will explained that each time their agency built a website for a nonprofit, he was amazed at how much their team members got out of the experience. Sure, the nonprofit was given a free website, but the people who worked on it felt a new pride in their skills. Rachel and Will had wanted to put on a big event to see if they could bring together volunteers to build a lot of nonprofit websites in a small period - maybe even a few dozen if they really went after it - but kept finding that to be too large of a concept.

"We recently decided to simply see if we could get one other agency to put a team together, and over a weekend, their team and ours would each build a website. If it works, maybe we'll try more. I think it has legs, but we'll see how that first experience goes."

He stood up, walked over to his backpack, and pulled out the envelope that Liz had given him on the day Charles had died. He looked down at it, holding it tightly with both hands.

"I think it's time I read this letter. I know, you're right; what's taken me so long? Sarah thinks it's because this letter represents the last thing you've ever said to me, and I'm afraid to officially say goodbye to you. She assures me that I'll still have you in my heart, and we can still 'talk' whenever I want. And she's usually right about these things, so . . . "

He took a deep breath and pulled the letter out of the envelope. He sat back down next to Charles's gravestone and unfolded the paper in his hands, immediately feeling a spark of sadness upon seeing Charles's distinctive handwriting.

It read:

Dear Will,

It took a while for you to read this letter, didn't it? You didn't wait more than a month, did you?

There are a few things I wanted to say to you that, well, I just wasn't able to get out. Perhaps it's because I was raised in a different era, but sharing emotions isn't something I've ever been particularly good at.

I want you to know how proud I am of you. The idea that you are struggling to figure out if you've made an impact with your work bothers me, because you absolutely have. Hopefully, the talks we had at the hospital reminded you of the power of dreaming small, and helped you to see yourself like I see you. At the very least, you've helped this old man more than you'll ever know.

Make sure Danni knows how proud I am of her as well, and don't you dare accidentally meet up with her on her graduation trip! I know you mean well, but this is meant to be a time for her to see the world and experience new things on her own. She can't do that with her dad following her around! She's an amazing kid, and we both know she'll be just fine.

You know, my purpose was to have an outsized, positive impact on the world. I hope I made a little bit of a dent in that direction, though there was still so much more I wish I could have done. Perhaps you can take on the mantle and make your own outsized, positive impact. One small dream at a time.

Your friend,
Charles

P.S. Reach out to Nick Andrews. Our conversations about finding meaning in one's work got me thinking I should record some audio on my journey to leading a more purposeful life. Nick gave me a recording device, and each day, I recorded parts of my story. Maybe the two of you can cobble that together into some kind of book project or something. Either way, he has the tapes and is awaiting your call.

Will folded the letter and put it back in the envelope. He wiped a tear from his eye and thought: I guess Charles wasn't done talking to me after all.

PARTING THOUGHTS

Thank you for reading *Dream Small*. Sincerely and honestly, I appreciate you so much.

Whenever someone takes the time to read something I write, I see it as a minor miracle. The idea that I have something to say that even one person wants to hear is incredibly humbling.

As I mentioned in the Preamble, this book represents a shift in direction (less business, more 'life') and style (I played with a fourth-wall-breaking narrator and hope that worked for you).

This was also a much harder book to write because, well, as Sir Arthur Quiller-Couch wrote in his 1916 book *On the Art of Writing*, sometimes you have to "murder your darlings." Having Charles die was no easy task, as he represents several people in my life who are *very* important to me (and who, thankfully, are still very much alive, continuing to do their best to stop me from running headfirst into walls).

I love the character of Charles, so that was tough.

All my books draw from my personal experiences, but I'm typically fairly covert in how I write about them. I change names or mix around stories, and you kind of have to have experienced them with me to know who or what I am talking about.

This book, however, brings real-life people to the forefront, and I want to take a moment to recognize them.

Stanley Raff is loosely based on Stan Rapp. Stan, like Stanley, is an ad guy, a legendary one at that, but there the similarities end. I wanted to include Stan because I respect him so much, and he was a major partner in getting my first book, *The 5-Day Turnaround*, out into the world.

Ashley is less loosely based on Ashley Jones, founder and CEO of Momento. She's an incredible human, and you can learn more about her and Momento at momentofoundation.org.

Nick Andrews is a combination of Andrew Vogel (try to catch him not smiling) and Nicole Wedekind, my partners at Ripples Media. That was fun.

The author Nick works with to write the biracial books is based on Ekaette Kern and her children's book, *The Colors of Me: A Journey of Identity for Biracial Children*, which belongs on every kid's shelf.

The beginning of 48in48 is discussed as part of Will and Rachel's efforts to do more good (similar to my and Adam Walker's efforts back in 2015.) If you aren't aware of 48in48, you should be: 48in48.org

Everyone who knows me is aware that Charles's purpose, to have an outsized, positive impact on the world, is my personal purpose. We'll see if Will embraces the same purpose . . . something tells me he will. My hope is that this book helps you lead a more fulfilling life and that you find your way to doing more purposeful work.

If you ask me, we all want more meaning in our lives. We want to feel a sense of purpose and impact and to know we're making a positive difference. And we all have different dreams on how to accomplish that. In most cases, our dreams begin as the classic BHAGs - big, hairy, audacious goals. This book is my way of saying that's a mistake.

Everyone will say you should dream big and swing for the fences, and in fact, I used to use those exact words. But I've come to learn that dreaming BIG just might be what's holding us back from pursuing our dreams.

We can use our gifts, or as I call them, our superpowers, to do good . . . and we can change our lives and, in some cases, the world. Only we have to have *manageable* dreams and goals. We must stop believing that our contribution is too small to be meaningful and instead think *even smaller*.

So the next time you have that feeling inside that your work doesn't matter, or you're feeling unfulfilled and underwhelmed by your impact on the world, do me a favor . . . think about your dream, make it a little smaller, and then get to work.

The world is counting on you.

ACKNOWLEDGMENTS

First and foremost, the team at Ripples Media-Andrew Vogel, Nicole Wedekind, and DMF (yes, I get to call her that) - for being the best publishing team a person could work with. This team works so hard and always with a smile on their faces, and it's my absolute honor to be able to work with them.

My internal editing crew that read this manuscript before I kicked it off to the professionals at Ripples: my wife Emily and my sisters, Jennifer and Kelly. Thanks for your effort, honesty, and support in getting this book ready.

Jacqui Chew, for asking me to speak at TEDx and helping me arrive at and refine the idea of dreaming small.

Kemie Nix, for helping me realize that a person truly can be at peace when dying.

I feel the need to point out that Stephen King (through interviews and his book, *On Writing*) and Brandon Sanderson (through his interviews and the classes he teaches) have taught me so much about writing. They remain my writing idols and I'm forever appreciative that they find it in their hearts to help other writers.

My mentors along the way for giving me the idea of Charles many years ago when I started writing my first book. And while Charles represents a handful of people, he mostly represents Ken Bernhardt. I'm not sure where I'd be or what I'd be doing if it weren't for you, Ken. I'm forever in your debt.

And as always, to my amazing family, the 7mires: Emily, Zac, Drew, Kaitlyn, Hannah, and Kai. As lucky as I've been, and I've been incredibly lucky so many times, I'll always count my blessings that I have you all in my life.

ABOUT THE AUTHOR

JEFF HILIMIRE is the bestselling author of *The Turnaround Leadership Series* and an accomplished entrepreneur who has launched multiple organizations and successfully sold two companies. He is currently a Partner at Purpose Group, a purpose-driven holding company focused on bringing PVTV to organizations across the United States. He is currently the Board Chair at Dragon Army, an award-winning digital engagement company, as well as the founder of Ripples Media.

Hilimire is also the co-founder and board member of two nonprofit organizations. 48in48 is a global nonprofit that produces hackathon events, building 48 nonprofit websites in 48 hours. The A Pledge creates a path for systemic opportunity in Atlanta by inspiring marketing and advertising agencies to commit to matching the diversity of their team to that of our city by 2030.

Jeff lives in Atlanta with his wife Emily and their five children. You can follow Jeff's adventures on his personal blog, jeffhilimire.com, or sign up for his newsletter at jeffhilimire.com/newsletter.

Other Titles from The Turnaround Leadership Universe (TLU)

Learn how to grow your business or team by leading like an entrepreneur. This book will help you embrace a startup mentality to create transformative growth.

Leading a successful business is hard enough, and it's even harder during an emergency. This book will help you thrive even in times of crisis, and become stronger as a result.

Can a shared Purpose unlock your organization's best work? Using insights from PVTV and The Great Game of Business, this book will enable teams to reach their full potential.

Culture is routinely cited as one of the main reasons organizations find success. But what is an undeniable culture? This book will help you jumpstart growth in the face of competition and other obstacles.

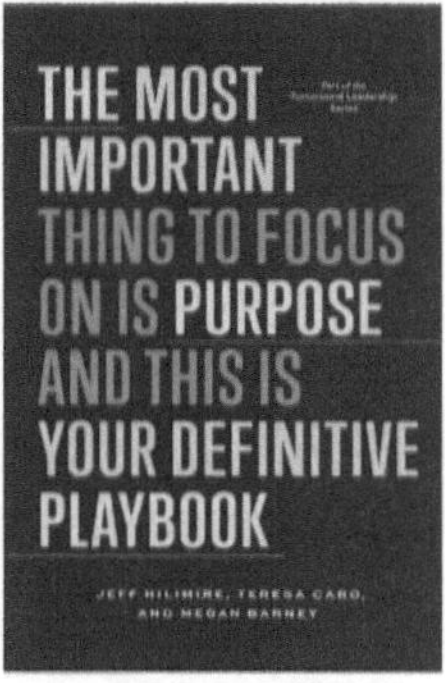

Want the playbook on how to develop develop purpose-driven leadership? This book provides leaders with an actionable plan and facilitation guide to execute on building a purpose-driven team and culture.

9 798991 387033